The chaos of things

Leah Faye

BookLeaf Publishing
India | USA | UK

Presentation by *BookLeaf Publishing*

Web: www.bookleafpub.com

E-mail: info@bookleafpub.com

ISBN: 978-93-5744-405-7

First edition 2022

DEDICATED

to my feeling brain

no passing in the night

a person who truly values you would never put you in a position to lose you, but it's easier said than done,
as I watched you drift
away

all I could do was stand there and stare,
and watch the ships
sail away to another place
at a different pace
That I could never keep up with

sewing class

words will
tear the threads from your
    skin
and it will only be in that moment
that you will you realize

- you never learnt to sew.

shameful behaviour

& with a heart like yours
what a shame for those who lost it

- an embarrassment

honesty

you gotta speak the truth even if your voice
shakes and the ground crumbles beneath you and
you feel your bones rip apart like paper in water
and your eyes turn into waterfalls
because
the truth is better
    than any words that aren't

Shakespeare would be proud

and all at once
and all so suddenly
the spark we had completely disappeared
and something that was once called magic
turned into something tragic

- Disney lied.

laika

don't let someone hunt down your lion heart and murder it
just for another trophy on their wall

trust in the universe

maybe it's all in the plan,
to create cracks in souls
and allow the rains to come pouring down

- all for it to let those beautiful flowers grow
through

freefall

there are some days that I find myself
feeling a little bit lonely
I take a second to remember all the people I let
go of, just to make space for myself

and I feel a little bit less lonely and a little bit
more proud of how far I've come because at
least when it feels like no one has my back,
I know I have my own

unapologetically chaotic

I can no longer break myself
To be smaller and more demure

I am not soft-spoken.
I am not reserved or easy to please

I must take up all of the space I can
or the walls
will close in on me
with too much pressure

and then much like a star,

    I will collapse

10/20 vision

my eyes are always wide open,
but I know that I see better with my heart

- a break or two is worth it

journey for 1

how grateful I am
that amidst all the chaos and confusion
the growing and the falling
that I’ve managed to realize that the space that
felt empty in between my fingers
can now be filled by holding my own hand

- with deep content in my own whole self

death do us part

do not reach for me with someone else's name
on the tip of your tongue
I am not a sometimes, or a quick fix
I am an always

- all's well that ends

finally, unconditional

there's no perfect version of me
I spent years trying to make up for parts I was missing
little did I know,
I was already so whole
I don't need a perfect version of me
it's time to love my whole self

- I'm done waiting for a reason to

to let

if you push me away,
I won't stay here
when you finally decide that I'm worth it,
I'll be gone already
when you say that you know I'm important to you,

I won't be here
I don't have what it takes
to be an open house for broken souls,

not anymore
you might think I'm not,
but I know

I'm worth it

grounded roots

and I deeply know
in my heart
there are finally flowers blooming again

- here comes the spring

cartoon on a loop

always dancing between the line of chasing
feelings and running away from them

- Tom & Jerry emotional chase

a simple life lesson I have yet to learn

you will usually find yourself
in the place you avoid going

- out of your comfort zone

what fate really means

I miss your presence in moments that do not yet exist

- meant to meet, but never meant to be

anger attacks the owner

forgive, forgive, forgive
not for them,
but for yourself
because in the end the only person carrying
the weight of the vendetta

will be you

self-loathe

it is exhausting to know,

I have hurt myself
way more

than any of you fuckers could

-it still didn't stop them trying

clear as crystal

everything or nothing,
that is how I tend to live
no in-between meeting point
there is no space or give

I exist purely outside of the grey area
there's no confusion or contradiction
you're either fully in

or

you're just
            cut out

www.ingramcontent.com/pod-product-compliance
Lightning Source LLC
Chambersburg PA
CBHW051722130826
49812CB00034B/1301
9789357444057